THE LOVE OF A
COLD, WET, NOSE

THE LOVE OF A COLD, WET, NOSE

STORIES OF A HOSPICE DOG

Stuart P. Stofferahn

ISBN-10: 1979525234
ISBN-13: 9781979525237

DEDICATION

To Mike

CONTENTS

ACKNOWLEDGMENTS

Finding the right words to properly encapsulate the gratitude for so many people is perhaps the most difficult part of writing a book.

My family. All of you. Thank you.

Heather, who has read this book at least a dozen times and never rolled her eyes once at the repeated requests.

Pat and Denise for your editing expertise.

So many friends for the encouragement and votes of confidence.

INTRODUCTION

DYING PEOPLE WANT you to know something.

They want you to know that you are going to die someday too. This is obviously not news to you, but what if that day were today? In fact, what if it happened right now? Would that matter to you? Would that be news to you?

If your life ended right now – right this second – what would your legacy be? Who would remember you? What would they say? Dying people want you to know that everything you are stays behind not only in the lives of people you have loved, but also in those whom you have neglected.

They want you to know that you are defined by the love you give. Nothing more, nothing less. They also want you to know that we overcomplicate love. In reality, it is a pretty simple act. I have witnessed it over and over again.

When I began this journey, I only knew that Buckley needed to be shared. What follows in this book is what I have learned and, more importantly, how I have incorporated those lessons into my life.

Most of the poems I have written are related to our hospice experiences, but some are reflections on my own life as I have lived it. However, all of them have been given a voice from our hospice clients; they have taught me how silly it has been to keep the words hidden simply because of fearful judgment (this was made QUITE clear to me by one client who chastised me for keeping the poems to myself – "you were not made just for you," she said). And of course, it was Buckley who gently persuaded me to share him with the world that has given all of this a starting point. And even he, who is eight and a half at the writing of this book, looks up at me with his ever-whitening face and reminds me that his time on this earth is limited to a very few more years. I hear him tell me every day . . . *Do not waste a second of it.*

I recall many years ago when my youngest son, Paul, was around seventeen years old, and he was asked to write a poem in his English Literature class. He was struggling, and not just because he didn't like English Literature. We talked about why it was such a struggle. The conversation shifted to the poetry he had read and the feelings behind the poems. They were laced with emotion – mostly heartache - and this was the key. He was seventeen years old, and he had not yet experienced struggle or suffering that brought words to paper.

Except, he had.

I asked him if he remembered the day we had to put Comet down. Comet was our golden retriever we adopted when Paul was four. He was the first dog Paul really knew, and spent the next eleven years with us as his best friend. When we made the decision to put Comet down, he could barely walk. I asked Paul if he wanted to be there; he told me that Comet had been by his side for eleven years, and he needed to be with him now. It was a very courageous decision for a fifteen-year-old. Comet was surrounded by family – Paul and I on the floor beside him and family filling the room. As anyone who has experienced putting down a beloved family pet, it was heart-wrenching – even to this day.

For months, Paul struggled and would wake up in the middle of the night missing Comet. While the heartbreak would eventually ease, he never forgot the pain of saying goodbye to such a loyal and loving companion. While he certainly loves his mom and me (and his brother, if he *had* to admit it), a boy and his dog have an attachment that is unexplainable.

Suddenly, writing a poem was no longer difficult for Paul.

Such as it has been with me. While it is true that we will have to say goodbye to each hospice client we serve, the "death" part of the process comes when it comes, and until that moment, our service is about living. I think you will find that theme running throughout this book. Certainly there is sadness but only because of the love that was shared in the time we had together.

It seems fitting that we begin with a trilogy about time. As I was writing the poem *One Second*, a young man walked slowly in front of me. He was in a body brace and was using a walker. I estimate he was in his early twenties, and I can only guess that the young man had been injured in an accident of some sort (or combat since we were on a military installation). He was accompanied by a young lady, presumably his spouse or girlfriend, and her mom who drove up to meet them for lunch. They took up a table near me.

As anyone who has lived through a similar situation of a serious accident or injury, we soon discover that we are either 1) in a crisis, 2) leaving a crisis, or 3) preparing for our next crisis. Unless you are a hobbit living by yourself on the side of a hill in the middle of nowhere, to some extent, you have family, friends, or loved ones who surround you daily. And when we consider the incredible limitations of the control we actually have in this world, it's a wonder crisis doesn't visit us more regularly.

Crisis is both a blessing and a curse. As with this young man, it offers an opportunity for family to come together in a way that cultivates closeness where it may not have existed before – thus strengthening resiliency. Almost immediately, priorities become re-aligned, we realize what is important in this world, and we adjust accordingly – at least temporarily. As this young man continues to recover and heal, there is a good chance that the memories of the crisis will fade, priorities relax, and family, friends and loved ones will go back to a routine that existed prior to the crisis. Therein lies the curse.

Our reaction to crisis is largely dependent on how we have prepared for it. Unlike preparing for a football game, we typically don't continually practice scenarios of crises thrust upon us. And even if we did, the difference between talking through a scenario and living it can be as different as night and day. Instead, our reaction takes shape by naturally reaching out to loved ones in our time of need – or when crises strike. So, our "preparation" lies in how we have lived our lives and how we have treated people. If you expect others to be there for you, you need to be there for others.

As we know, crisis doesn't always have a happy ending – at least with respect to everyone living happily ever after. But it does offer continued poignancy if we allow it to speak to us. *One Second, Time,* and *Time II* have been sixteen years in the making. They have undergone an equal number of starts, re-writes, and throwaways as I have continued my dance with the meaning of time, and our incredible capacity to take it for granted. In these poems, you will read about someone who has lost a brother to a tragic car accident, a father who has comforted his son during a first heartbreak, a volunteer who has listened to people with terminal illnesses, an ex-husband who has mourned the loss of a marriage, a friend who has shared a glass of fine wine with a cancer survivor, and a new husband who has found love again.

I recall a conversation with one of my first hospice clients as we talked about her diagnosis and the meaning of time. We discussed Maggie Callahan's book, *Final Gifts* and the tragedy of wasted seconds. As my client paused and watched the second hand on the clock and the seconds ticking by, she looked at me and asked me a simple question.

"What are *you* doing with your seconds?"

It was a question that shook me to my core, and it immediately changed my world and how I interacted with it.

The seconds we have are sacred gifts that have been given to us to fulfill our potential - to leave a legacy. They account for the love we have experienced, the pain, the hope, the loneliness, the successes, the failures, the compassion, the forgiveness, and the celebrations that have come to pass and the ones yet to be. They also account for the fear in our lives that stops us from doing what it is that we have been called to do – which is tragic in the eyes of the universe.

Seconds have a way of flying under the radar as we continue to live our lives based upon assumption. Dying people would have us re-think our assumptions and ask us to start participating in our lives as if we only had six months *or less* to live. They want us to know that withholding forgiveness tops the list as the worst use of our seconds. Sustaining resentment is a close second. They also want us to know that there are some words that need to be used much more frequently – namely "I am sorry" and "I love you".

Just as I was asked the question, now I ask you.

What are *you* doing with *your* seconds?

ONE SECOND

We
Hardly
Notice
Them

Unless
One
Is
Required

And there
Are no more
To be
Spared

That's how
It goes
You
See

That
Which
We
Have

Is that
Which we
Take
For granted

Enlightenment
Is
The
Cure

But it
Comes
At
A cost

We
Are
A silly
Lot

TIME

More prose
About time
A love-hate
Relationship

Too much
Never enough
If only I had more
When will it pass?

Always living in the present
Forever hopeful of the future
Saddened by regrets
Of the past.

Forgetful of it in the midst
Of love.
A prison sentence
At love's loss.

Captured in photographs
Alive in the
Hands
Of a clock

Represented by wrinkles
Rings of the Oak Tree
Shapes of the Moon
And the Promise of Spring

Mortal enemy
To those who
Have been cheated
By terminal illness

A gift
For those
Who have survived
It

Longing for more
When silence replaces words left unspoken
And death claims the life
Of a loved one

Just one
Second more
To say
I love you.

TIME II

You
Are
A tricky
Bastard

A
Disappearing act
At life's
End

An uninvited
Unwanted guest
During
Heartbreak

And
Yet
You
Heal

With the
Gift
Of
Years

And the
Subtle presence
Of a
Butterfly

Allowing
Love to
Spring eternal
Once again

You
Are
A tricky
Bastard

OUR STORY

In the summer of 2009, I got a puppy. I named him Buckley. I simply wanted a companion – a buddy. I was in the beginning stages of divorce after being married for 14 years. Certainly, divorce is probably not a good reason to get a puppy, but I anticipated that there were few things on this planet that could fill those long and lonely hours like a puppy could. Of course, I was right. He is an English Golden Retriever, and he has all the papers to prove his pedigree. His blood runs feverish for the trail of gamebirds, but none of that interested me (and, as it turns out, does not interest him in the slightest). I have always loved dogs, and it had been quite some time since I had raised a puppy. I also wanted to teach my son how to raise a puppy, and the summer was the perfect time to do so.

Over time, I noticed Buckley's keen ability to connect with people – especially kids, although his focus has gradually shifted to connecting more closely to the elderly. When he was about four years old, he was on the deck of my house and there were three kids who called for him from a yard adjacent to mine. He ran off the deck, down the stairs, and up to the fence. However, as he approached, the kids ran away. They eventually came back, but the process was not lost on Buckley.

The very next day, the same kids called to him again, and I expected the process to repeat. This time as Buckley got about 20 feet away from the fence, he stopped, and he *crawled* up to the fence – and the kids didn't run away. The significance of his action was not lost on me. It was immediately apparent that this dog was special – and he needed to be shared. And so our journey began.

As I began searching for a place that would offer us the necessary training to become a therapy dog team, I came upon a local non-profit called Domesti-Pups. I contacted the Executive Director, Michelle O'Dea, and registered Buckley and I for the class to become certified. Upon our graduation and subsequent probationary period, we began our visits to elderly homes and assisted-living facilities. We would slowly go from room to room and stop for visits with anyone who wished to pet a dog; we were always popular.

It is estimated that up to 50% of assisted-living and nursing home residents never receive any visitors after they are admitted; the significance of these dog therapy teams cannot be over-stated. After a few months of doing these monthly visits, I felt something was missing. Our visits were short; each resident would have the opportunity to meet each team, but that meant that with 3-4 teams, the visits would be a few minutes each before we needed to move on to the next room. This may seem "rushed", and it is. However, it is mostly because we just don't have enough therapy teams to fill the need, and we want to make sure we get at least a few minutes with as many residents as we can.

After some reflection, I realized that it was the short visit time with each resident that created a gap for me. I needed more time to visit, to learn about who these people were, and what their lives were like. I wanted to know their hopes, dreams, challenges, and celebrations. I needed more depth. This was not a surprise to me, an introvert, as I tend to seek out conversations with individuals and smaller groups to talk about things that make life worth living.

As I was drinking coffee one morning and contemplating how I could fulfill the needs of clients in addition to my own, I turned the paper to a full-page ad by a local elderly services provider whose focus was hospice care. In retrospect, this was not the first time in my life that the universe was so obvious in its attempt to wake me up and present an opportunity. However, I am a slow learner. I remember the ad very specifically, and I remember the moment. I remember turning the page while at the same time asking myself, "If there was just some place we could serve that would allow me to develop deeper relationships with clients . . . "

Luckily for me, the light bulb came on. I called the phone number listed. I asked if they had a dog therapy program available for hospice clients, and I was directed to Susan Eichele, who at the time was the Director of Hospice Volunteers. Little did either of us know that we would become life-long friends as we navigate this world. She told me that while their organization had at one time operated with dog therapy teams, there were none currently. I asked if she would be willing to meet Buckley (no one can turn down Buckley) and sit down to talk about the possibility of re-starting the program. As of the writing of this book, that was four years ago and over 400 hours of volunteer service . . . and counting.

I'm pretty sure that Michelle O'Dea had no idea what she was getting into when she allowed me to become part of Domesti-Pups. Here's this guy who goes around town extending service commitments to organizations and leaving her to pick up the pieces by dotting all the "i's" and crossing all the "t"s. Even with the reading of this book, she is rolling her eyes. I could write another book focusing solely on the mission of Domesti-Pups and Michelle, but I will leave that for you to discover on your own. It will be worth your time.

From the moment we began our visits with hospice clients, my life was transformed. This book is an attempt to reflect this transformation through the life experience of the clients, the wisdom they wished to pass along, and my experiences sitting in conversation and in quiet reflection. The poems I have shared are described in the narration that follows. They are a reflection of my experiences with my clients, but with the additional perspective of the life I have lived and the person I wish to become.

A LESSON LEARNED

A CALLING

It is
A
Daunting
Task

For which
Most
Never
Accomplish

Some
Fail
To
Begin

Lacking the
Courage
To vanquish
The fear

And allow
The light
From
Within

To give
Permission for others

To do
The same

Who do
You suppose
You
Are?

What many things
Has the Universe
Assigned
To you?

On a
Silver platter
They
Exist

Patience
Awareness
Urgency
Indeed . . . urgency

For you
Were not
Created
Just for you

If I had to list the single greatest lesson learned from my experience thus far, I would speak to the universal calling for us to fulfill our potential from people who are aware of their imminent death. This is a calling not only to seek out the passion that drives us, but also to take every opportunity to love deeply, act courageously, live graciously, apologize freely, and treat each other with compassion that knows no limits. We simply do not have time to do otherwise.

Poignancy is magnified in the lives of people who are dying. Everywhere, they are reminded of the things they used to take for granted – even simple things like green bananas (an actual discussion with a client). Have you ever contemplated whether you will live long enough to see them ripen? And yet, even in excellent health, there is no guarantee you will see them turn from green to yellow. In fact, there is nothing written anywhere that I will outlive the clients Buckley and I serve.

Before you take this all too literally, dying people don't want you to only buy ripened bananas. They also don't want you to interpret this as the excuse you need to quit your job, buy a Corvette, and go sky-diving. Further, it would be counterproductive to curl yourself up into a ball, turn out the lights and never again leave the house in fear of the full realization of what little you control. They want you to live life with the poignancy reflected in the knowledge of having six months or less to live, but in a way that reflects the legacy you wish to leave behind. And they will tell you that your legacy is written solely in the way in which you have treated people in your lifetime. When you are dying, this is the only thing that matters. However, *fixing* your legacy at that point is oftentimes too late. I have witnessed clients who have *clung to life* hoping for one last opportunity to reach out to someone with whom they had needed to resolve a conflict or apologize for something they had done. Such things should have been done *as they had lived life*, not as they were dying.

Generally speaking, dying people don't have a problem saying "I'm sorry" and "I love you". In fact, most of the clients I have served made the realization that these were words they had been *withholding* that were now said freely and often. Conversely, there were words that they *had been saying* that had now disappeared from their vocabulary. They would tell you that, if you feel like telling someone you love them, never miss the opportunity to do so. Say it often and without concern. Similarly, when it comes to saying "I'm sorry", never let a day go by without claiming responsibility for any part you may have played in any situation that requires acceptance and forgiveness. In other words, never wait to say, "I'm sorry".

All of these things are components of unrealized potential. We limit ourselves due to a number of factors, both societal and personal, whether we take others' opinions as those of our own, or we stop ourselves from pursuing dreams because we don't fit the part. Maybe we wait to forgive because of the power we think we may hold over someone, or we simply think that we don't have time for whatever it is the universe may be pointing us toward. Part of my own personal transformation was a renewed – or better yet, awakened – sense of awareness. It is not a stretch to say that most of us walk through this life very self-centered, and I count myself among this crowd. Within this realm, our vision is mostly centered on what this world has to offer *me*. Oftentimes, this means that we expect things to happen for us, to us, or about us – severely limiting anything we may have to offer *to* the world.

My transformation opened my eyes to a universe that provides opportunities *for* us, but it is up to us whether or not we see them as such. It is also up to us to do the work necessary to fulfill the opportunity. When an opportunity is a *passion*, the work is secondary to the potential that exists beyond it. Therein lies the *realized* potential. Just remember, if you expect it to be easy, you will never find the awareness necessary to begin the journey.

I could have simply seen Buckley's connection with those kids as "cute", gone back inside and continued my day as planned. Instead, the first thing I did was to stop for a moment to realize that something special was happening and that I was witnessing it. I allowed the curiosity to fill me and let the love, compassion, and grace lead me. Very often (as in my case), this means sacrifice will be involved – your time, your money, etc. – and you will have to decide whether or not the sacrifice is worth it.

When I speak of the "universe", I speak in terms of whatever you believe to be your "higher being", "energy", "light", or "God", etc. This is for you to determine. The universe has brought to me a new awareness of not only the opportunities, but also of the world around me and the people in it. I walk more softly, speak more clearly, and take far less for granted. I also still make mistakes, but I have found that I move more quickly toward forgiveness, both of myself and others. Every Monday morning spent with my clients renews this sense of awareness as I share sacred seconds with people who teach and inspire me - and who wish to do the same with you.

I do not believe we are somehow "penalized" for passing on an opportunity that presents itself. Quite honestly, I don't believe the universe particularly cares what is going on in our lives. It doesn't care about the plans we have made, the money in our bank accounts, the trips we have taken, or the people we know. It only cares about the existence of potential and our ability to take advantage of it. To some, the path is illuminated quite quickly; for others, it takes many opportunities to finally awaken. Sadly for most, the potential goes unrealized.

I have found that taking advantage of opportunities does require a good bit of faith in a higher being, but certainly more faith in yourself. Think of the high-ranking CEO of a very successful organization who ditched everything to make flutes out of bamboo (true story, by the way). To some it was a mid-life crisis. To others it was an opportunity to fulfill potential. To the person making the flutes, it made no difference what others thought, because it made complete sense to her. And the universe is happy, because she is fulfilling the potential that exists inside of her. Fulfilling potential requires one simple step: Do something. You just have to not care what others think while you are taking the risk and making the sacrifice. I can assure you that there was much guffawing over the CEO leaving a successful firm to make bamboo flutes. However, I am quite sure that the former CEO is very happy doing what she has been given the opportunity to do and is making a fine living doing it, because she is passionate about it. Her success is determined by how *she* measures it, not by how others judge it. She is fulfilling her potential.

And so we come to this book and my journey. I can assure you that twenty years ago – even five years ago – I had no intention of public speaking as a means of putting food on the table. Writing a book was nowhere in my thoughts. My plan was to finish my doctorate and eventually become a superintendent of a public school district somewhere in Nebraska. Having completed my master's degree in 2010, it was a progression that – if I didn't continue right away – I knew I would never start.

Two years into my doctoral coursework, Buckley decided to send me the message that he needed to be shared, and the universe would not be ignored. This is not to say that I didn't try to ignore it. Working a full-time job, going to night class, writing papers, and already volunteering in the community, my argument for ignoring it would have been sound - I'm *already* doing *enough*. However, with the image of him crawling up to those kids in my head, there was no deflecting the message. Remember, the universe doesn't care about your money, your plans, or what you think you *want* to do. It only cares about presenting opportunities. Buckley and I would pursue, and the universe would rejoice once again.

Interestingly enough, when our training was over and after our volunteering began, the urgency of completing my doctorate only intensified. I pursued it with a laser focus but without ignoring the part of my life that was most important – my family. My rationale for this urgency was that there was obviously a school district out there somewhere that needed me *desperately*.

Somehow, I was able to fit it all in although my family and friends would tell you today that they don't know how I did it. When asked, my response was always the same. It always came down to me asking a question of myself, "What am I doing with my seconds?" I have never exercised stronger, studied harder, or pursued with more passion than the hour after our Monday morning hospice visits. That inspiration would continue throughout the week without dissipation. I found that I would schedule events, commitments, and even vacations around my Monday mornings. Certainly, my clients depended on these visits, but *I* also depended on *them* for inspiration.

As I was beginning what would be the second-to-last last year of my doctoral work, I went to visit my cousins in Wisconsin for no particular reason other than to stop ignoring the fact that we had grown apart. It was time to fix that (what was I doing with my seconds?). One of my cousins, Cindy, has a son, Kyle, who is adopted from Russia. After some years, it became apparent that he suffers from the effects of fetal alcohol syndrome which presents a lot like autism. Kyle has the most difficulty with the social aspects of life, in addition to some curricular challenges. During our conversation, Cindy said that she did not know what would become of Kyle when she dies. Read that again. Not when he *graduates*, or when he gets married, or when he hits any other milestone in his life – but when *she dies*. For Kyle and every other kid who is not "neuro-typical", the support they receive in a public school stops once they graduates or age out of the school system. Once that occurs, Cindy will have to seek support from the state which oftentimes means long waiting lists. As in most cases, service-eligible candidates like Kyle far outnumber the state's ability to provide service support.

Prior to that conversation, my doctoral thesis statement was firm: "Mitigating the effects of poverty on student achievement." In fact, prior to my trip to Wisconsin, I had largely completed three of five chapters. My seven-hour trip home was driven in absolute silence, mostly because I began internalizing the tremendous burden Cindy was carrying, and partly because I was mourning the death of my thesis at the time. The universe had struck again. I would go on to graduate with the doctoral theses titled "Becoming independent: Employer practices that enhance success for employees with an autism spectrum disorder." In addition to walking away from a dissertation that was three-fifths complete, I would begin to think about practical actions we could take to improve the outlook for kids and adults with an autism spectrum disorder and other learning differences. The picture was becoming clearer that my increased pace in completing my doctorate had nothing to do with serving a public school. I began conversations with friends and colleagues as soon as I arrived home. These conversations have led to the developmental stages of creating a practical learning environment through the non-profit Nebraska Transition College (NTC) – a three-year program that empowers individuals to live independently through employment and community support systems. Certainly the universe has found a rube in me. As you will later read, during the course of all my studies, I had applied for numerous principal positions and even a superintendent position. While I had been close in several instances, I had never been selected. I was now discovering why.

The universe was just doing what it does. It was providing me opportunities to fulfill my potential – nothing more, nothing less. It was only through the poignancy of my hospice visits that

I was allowed the awareness necessary to see that my visit with Cindy presented an opportunity and ignited a fire. But following this path does not come without risk. For me, building this college meant abandoning my pursuit of a public school administrative position for which I had pursued a doctorate in Educational Leadership. After sixteen years of pursuit, to change course now seemed *ludicrous*. NTC was a dream - nothing more than an idea; a superintendent position was tangible. NTC offered no employment and no paycheck while we built the framework. There was no guarantee it would work. A superintendency offered salary and benefits there for the taking. Creating NTC meant building everything from the ground up. We would need a board, programs, curriculum, policies, development and money. A school district is already established, and it is supported by tax dollars. NTC meant great personal sacrifice; a superintendency would be a professional peak. The direction seemed clear enough.

I continued on my track to finish my doctorate and to pursue a superintendent position. I was even offered an interview for a small school district in Nebraska – and you will find out later how that turned out. But as I continued, the spark of NTC soon grew into a roaring fire, and it was all I could think about. I knew I had to make a decision, but I was fighting the fear with all my might.

What if I try and fail? After all, I have no idea what I was doing. I have never *built a college*. I have never built a board, built a curriculum, developed programming, or filed for non-profit status. I have organized fund raising to the tune of $2,000-3,000 but never $1.3 million! The fear behind the questions was easy to recognize, and it was a loud, steady voice. I also knew that fear was just the first stage of courage. I just had to move through it and have faith that what was on the other side was something incredible.

And then, other questions took over. What if I try and *succeed*? What if I share the message and find others who will help? What if we build a curriculum that becomes the gold standard for others to emulate? What if we find a way for these kids and adults to experience the same feeling you and I have by becoming fully involved in the community in which they live? What if Cindy no longer had to anguish over the thought of what would become of Kyle *after she died*?

With the inspiration of a cold, wet, nose and the clients we have served, I have dedicated myself to making Nebraska Transition College come to life. It is a story that is unfolding. My fear, while still real and present, has faded; it has loosened its grip. I believe this is partly due to the mission of what we are trying to accomplish, and partly because I have an incredible family backing me, and a board that is second to none. But again, it does not come without sacrifice. At of the writing of this book, there is no paid job that awaits me, and there is no *guarantee* that NTC will become a reality. But there *is* a guarantee that it *won't* unless we try.

My seconds are ticking by. *Your* seconds are ticking by. How are they being used?

The day I was asked that question, everything changed.

A LEGACY

LITTLE VOICE

It is silent
But
It speaks
Volumes

It is ever-present
And points
True
North

It has
The patience
Of
Job

And the
Urgency
Of
Disaster

It can be
Ignored
But it will not
Be silenced

Truth and love
Are its
Weapons
And armament

It laughs
At us
As we struggle
To outsmart it

And comforts
Us when
We come
To its terms

It asks only
That
We
Listen

So that
It
May lead
The way

Everything we do becomes part of what we choose to leave behind when we die. All of our choices are rooted either in love or fear. While most of what is happening around us remains outside our control, we still retain the ability to affect change. However, most of us choose to either ignore the opportunities that present themselves or fail to acknowledge that we are powerful beyond measure. Instead, we remain firmly entrenched in what we see as our own inadequacies – allowing them to dictate what we do, or maybe more significantly, what we don't do. In other words, we are afraid. Marianne Williamson addresses this perfectly in her book, "Everyday Grace". She instructs that "when we let our light shine, we unconsciously give permission for others to do the same" and "when we liberate the fear that is within us, our mere presence liberates others."

While we draw breath, we have the power to affect our legacy. When we are dead, our legacy becomes cemented in time. The choices we make lead to the legacy we leave behind. They reflect the priorities in our lives. Each person has the ability to discover what those priorities are. Some find a heading early in life and seem to be called for a singular purpose. Others need time to discern what that purpose is and oftentimes find themselves with many stops and starts. I am in the latter category, and at age 48 with many mistakes and false-starts, I am just beginning to find my footing. Still, the universe celebrates the fact that I have finally begun to uncover the potential that exists within my control. I am finally waking up to the opportunities that are presenting themselves, and the awareness of the world around me.

This has led to a heightened consciousness of the sheer barrage of choices we face on a daily basis. We choose constantly, and oftentimes without realizing the second and third-order effects they have on the world around us. Authors have expounded on the Butterfly Effect, which origin dates to Ed Lorenz in1969. He absorbed ridicule as he proposed that the wings of a butterfly, when in motion, move molecules – which move more molecules, and more molecules. If left undisturbed, eventually, these molecular movements could form a hurricane on the other end of the earth. While he was mostly dismissed in 1969, the theory was eventually proven correct. It now has its own position in the annuls of physics as the "Law of Sensitive Dependence upon Initial Conditions". The wings of one butterfly *have* the power to initiate a hurricane. Amazing.

This brings us back to you and me and the choices we make or the molecules we choose to move. Think back to a time when someone in your life offered advice or an opportunity. This person may have been a teacher, a friend, a parent, or even a stranger at a very curious time in your life. Because of that advice or encouragement at that moment, the trajectory of your life changed – however slightly or dramatically. Stephen Covey would liken a slight trajectory change to a "trim-tab" – the very small component on a boat's rudder that allows for very small changes in a heading initially resulting in huge changes thousands of miles away. The decisions we make at any given point in our lives can have enormous positive impacts or negative consequences years down the road.

If we break down the process, choices happen between a stimulus and response. Stimuli are everywhere. As stated before, each day we have the opportunity and responsibility to react to these stimuli, keeping in mind that even a non-reaction is still a reaction. It sounds simple, but it is actually a very complex string of events that can have enormous positive – and negative - impacts on our lives and the lives of those around you.

Take, for example, a situation with which we are all familiar – getting cut off in traffic. If we allow ourselves to think of that exact moment, we can actually feel our blood pressure begin to rise. We tend to immediately determine that the act was done premeditatively (on purpose). Of course, this situation demands an immediate response. A number of options pop into our mind. For some, it might involve speeding up to ride the bumper. Others might give the one-finger wave or decide to get in front of them and cut *them* off.

Time out.

Inside our brain lives a tiny gland called the amygdala. It's about the size of a shelled walnut, and it is responsible for our emotions in our responses. If we let it take control, we can easily find ourselves emotionally hijacked. That is to say if something triggers it, and we are not prepared, it's off to the races. Accounts have been given in which people have explained that they didn't know what they were doing. It was almost as if they were having an out of body experience - watching things unfold without any control. This happens because we are either unaware of the things that trigger this emotional response, or we have not developed tools for controlling it. We must harness it for a more appropriate response.

Let's keep going with the scenario.

Suppose that you've given in to the calling of your amygdala, and made the decision to cut off the other driver. Similarly, suppose his response is also emotional. When both of you come to a stoplight, suppose he gets out of his car and comes up to your door as you get out to confront him. He is yelling and you are yelling. He pulls out a gun and you pull out a gun. Before you know it, five people are lying bleeding on the sidewalk.

Silly?

Consider the former Florida police officer who confronted a fellow movie-goer seated in front of him. The former officer was angry that the man was texting and asked him to stop. The man didn't stop. The obvious next step was for the former police officer to fatally shoot him. True story.

As we peel back the onion, both scenarios have stimuli and responses. In between the stimuli and responses are the choices we make – the building blocks to the legacy we build and eventually leave behind. Could you ever imagine yourself in a similar situation as the two presented here? As we analyze the scenarios, I am quite certain that you would never consider pulling a gun and shooting a movie-goer over texting or allowing a situation to escalate to the point of shooting innocent people on the sidewalk. I am even more certain of the fact that the former Florida law enforcement officer considered himself in the same light. In other words, whether we want to admit it or not, we all have the *capacity* to allow our emotions to control the choices we make and the responses we carry out. Fortunately, there are some tools that we can utilize to help us build a better legacy.

GRACE

GRACE

Frustratingly
Random
In times
Of necessity

As much
Absent
As it is
Observed or acted upon

Consistency
A
Constant
Challenge

The act
Of loving kindness
Brings
Awareness

Not
A pat
On
The back

Triggered
By a sense
Of
Injustice

Or by
A calling
To
Servanthood

Listening
To the softening
Of
Your heart

In the
Midst
Of a
Justifiable response

Small acts
That
Change
The world

If the decisions we make now have the potential for such enormous consequences down the road – for us and for so many – it should give us pause as we consider our process for making such impactful choices. This is where the magic of grace comes in to focus. Philip Gulley has the most comprehensive definition of grace I have ever read. He defines it this way: "Grace, since it is not instinctive, begins with mindfulness, and our deliberate intention to act with loving kindness when we could have justifiably done otherwise."

If we can apply grace or insert it into our decision-making routine, the entire world would change before our eyes. There is an enormous amount of stimuli over which you hold no sway (initially anyway). Grace is not much concerned with that. Where grace does come into play and potentially holds a prominent place in your life and the lives of those close to you is how it is inserted into your decision-making process. In intentionally doing so (as Gulley's definition suggests), you will find that decision making changes from the under-observed, mundane, subconscious into ever-widening, life-changing, enriching opportunity for loving kindness – however small the decisions may be.

In practical terms, let's look at a simple act of grace and break down the definition.

Let's say you are walking into a building, and you observe that it appears someone will be walking in behind you. Depending on how you were raised, where you were raised, and the morals instilled within you, you may or may not hold the door for that person. But the bottom line is that holding the door for the person behind you is *not instinctive.* Subconsciously, we think of ourselves first. If a group of strangers was suddenly confronted by a hungry lion, the only concern would be to have the ability to outrun just one other stranger. The instinct is, even if only for a nanosecond, to walk through the doorway without holding the door for the person behind you.

Additionally, nowhere is it codified that a person must hold the door. You won't find it in any (credible) law books, and while social norms may dictate it, you won't go to jail or pay a fine for not performing the act. To hold the door, you must first acknowledge the instinct (be mindful of it) and *intentionally* act counterintuitively – sort of an override. Despite our best efforts to continue down the path of gracious behavior, it is important to note that this moment of intentionally overriding instinct is the pivotal point at which we begin to fail in our attempts – more on that later.

As you continue, you have overridden your own self-centered instinct, and you hold the door, even though nowhere does it say you must. You have *deliberately intended* to act with *loving kindness,* and you feel pretty darn good about doing so (and you should!). You could have easily justified the opposite response – late to a meeting, didn't see the person, or just plain didn't care. Depending on your moral compass, the decision to not hold the door may or may not affect you as you proceed with your day. But, even though all of this enters and leaves your mind in a split second, you have acted graciously, and you have met all conditions of Gulley's definition.

And then just as quickly, everything falls apart.

As the person walks through the doorway, he continues without saying "thank you". Almost immediately, the act itself turns from being an act for *someone* into an act for *you*, as your amygdala takes over and begins letting emotion run amok. Judgement of that person takes place as you consider how it is possible that someone could be so rude. You may even contemplate never holding the door again. Why should you if you won't *receive even a thank you* for *your* act of kindness. Suddenly, though the act itself still remains, the follow through has had a potentially devastating effect on any future acts of loving kindness, because it has now become about you.

The entire act of grace is initially built upon a very tender foundation. At several critical moments throughout this very quick process, we have to overcome our own ego and at every critical moment, the ego has the advantage. The key is to keep trying with continued acts of loving kindness. Eventually, the act itself is sufficient and a "thank you" is no longer in the thought process. It is important to note that the act itself has secondary and tertiary effects that you may never be witness to. Though you may have difficulty coming to grips with your own ego, the *act* is the molecule-mover. The person on the receiving end of the act may go on to perform the act himself after having remembered your kindness from earlier in the day. So, while we work on our own egos privately and continue to see the world change before our eyes, the acts we perform publicly are the wings of butterflies in motion.

AWARENESS

AWARENESS

The speed
With which
Life
Passes

Forces us
To choose
Our words
Wisely

Forces us
To be aware
Of each numbered
Heartbeat

Creates sadness
With the realization
That there is always
Too much to do

Makes more poignant
The value
Of
Love

Urgently
Calls us
To
Forgive

Routinely
Makes fools
As we take
It for granted

Causes us to
Pause
In quiet
Contemplation

Makes
More precious
Sacred acts
Of grace

WALKING GENTLY

Full awareness
Causes us
To rethink our partnership
In this world

A stranger
Is
No longer
Unknown

He becomes
Unimaginable potential
Forever Linked
To Our destiny

Memories
Are
Not just
Things of the past

As much as they are
Actions
Of
The present

A
Destination
No longer
Guides us

As does
The Journey
Which begs
Our participation

Fall, spring
Or a dog
Or a cat
Or a partner

Become
Spirits
Walking gently upon the earth
Aware

Allowing the spider
To cross
In front of us
Unharmed

These two poems were written a year apart, but are closely related. I remember the moment I became more consciously aware of what it meant to be part of the bigger picture. I was on a routine jog, and a spider was on the sidewalk directly in my path. While I still have an irrational fear of them today, I altered my path, so I would not harm it. I did not alter my path because of fear; I altered it because I did not want to cause harm. If you are a runner, you constantly look for things to occupy your brain while attempting to run a certain time, course, or pace. This was the first time I let a big bug alter my course, although by just one little step. That little alteration occupied my brain for the rest of the run. A bug? Really??

In the beginning, the *only* reason I started running was so I could eat whatever I wanted, and it was awesome. Once I began my hospice visits, it became about much, much more. It became about taking care of my heart so that I could be around as long as possible within the confines of whatever I could control. It became about running *because I could.* It became about taking a larger part in the world in whatever way I could contribute with the seconds I have been given. It became about that spider in my path that was doing nothing but being a spider and whose purpose was being fulfilled without me interrupting it. Very quickly that little spider became representative of the bigger world around me.

Still, however noble, I fight the anti-running monster inside my brain that easily has 100 daily excuses that sometime come close to preventing me from hitting the trails. The best antidote – in fact one that is the running monster's kryptonite – rests with my Monday morning visits. When I am training for the half marathon every year, I try to schedule my long runs to take place right after my last visit. It is when I am at my highest level of inspiration, and any doubts I have while on the run are quick to pass. The thoughts always come back to . . . *because you can.*

It didn't surprise me, then, that I would have an emotional response when I had the opportunity to get an echocardiogram ultrasound. Every once in a great while, as I was running, my heartrate would get a little off-kilter. I became concerned when, after one episode, it was difficult to get it back to a regular heartbeat. So, in I went to take a look at my beating heart on a computer screen.

I was not prepared. I watched it beat in front of me. It was surreal, and I was overcome with emotion. I was a little embarrassed at the unexpected response, but the technicians in the room assured me that this was not the first time it had happened. The closest I have come to explaining it was that it was like seeing, for the first time, your very best friend who has been with you through it all. A friend who has remained hidden, unseen, and unwilling to take the credit for anything he has done to help you in this world. And once seen, an even stronger partnership was formed as we committed to take care of each other.

I have learned that increased awareness has added a heightened level of participation in the world around me as well as how I interact with it and how I am perceived. It has added dimensions of beauty that had not existed previously, but it has also added tremendous burdens. It has meant that while the beauty of the world has just been filled with color, there is an almost overwhelming amount of work to be done, so pick, and do.

RESPONSIBILITY AND SACRIFICE

EVERY ACT OF grace is paired with some degree of sacrifice. Continuing with gracious acts of kindness, if you pause to get the door for someone, it might mean that you will be that much later for a meeting, a spot further back in line, or perhaps losing out on the very last Cinnabon. If someone is texting in front of you, you may move to a different seat, potentially sacrificing a better movie-viewing experience. If someone cuts you off in traffic, you can immediately assume that it was done by *accident* rather than on purpose. You can acknowledge that becoming stranded behind a red light isn't the big deal it could have been. Whenever you perform a loving act of kindness, you are thinking of someone else's needs before your own. The definition itself suggests sacrifice. In war, a soldier throwing herself on a grenade performs the ultimate act of loving kindness or sacrifice. They are synonymous.

Your responsibility in any act of grace begins with a stimulus. If you witness someone drop a pencil on the floor in front of you, you now own the responsibility to act or not act. If you did not witness the pencil dropping to the floor, you have no responsibility to act. This is not too tough to understand, but to some, it offers cognitive dissonance too great to overcome. Consider the bystander effect. The bystander effect is a phenomenon in which individuals do not offer any means of assistance to someone when other people are present. The more bystanders there are, the *less likely* someone will help (sacrifice). This happens because with so many people around, we don't feel as personally responsible to help. It also happens because we are scared to get involved. In other words, we lack the courage to make the conscious decision to offer assistance because – you guessed it – we are thinking of ourselves first.

Sacrifice is not easy. It means giving of our time and our resources, and letting go of our ego. Letting go of our ego may be the most significant of these. Dying people will tell you that sacrifice for others is the only legacy to leave behind because it means that you have used your seconds for loving acts of grace instead of focusing solely on amassing wealth and material possessions. Both of these fade quickly after you die. In the years I have served as a hospice volunteer, never once have I heard regret from a client who made a decision to forego a job promotion (and less pay) to stay close to family. I have, however, held the hand of a wealthy client who died alone.

THE FIRST VISIT

MY DO NOT KNOWS

I do not
Know
What I have
To offer

But
I
Will
Give

I do not know
What
To
Say

But
My
Heart
Speaks

I do not know
If I have
Comfort
To give

But
My hand

Reaches
Out

The
Laughter
Surprises
Me

The
Heartbreak
Does
Not

I go
Because
I am
Called

I do
Because
I
Am needed

I
Have
Cast
Away

My
Do
Not
Knows

The hospice volunteer training Buckley and I received was brutal. Well, Buckley didn't need the training – it was obviously for
me - and it wasn't brutal in the sense that I had miles to run and
peaks to climb (that would be a cake-walk). I had to connect
with what it meant to be dying.

After I had completed the training, I felt like a new graduate – ready to use the skills that I had been taught but not really
any idea how to do so. In this line of volunteering, you either
have what it takes or you don't. You can't feign empathy; this
isn't for everyone. I didn't doubt my intimate knowledge of what
it meant to mourn the loss of a loved one, but I had never sat
across from someone who *knew* they were going to die. That was
still very discomforting to me even after the training.

Then, the e-mail came. It was an urgent call for volunteers
to offer respite care for a family who was holding vigil for their
mother. She had entered her final transition, but she was experi-
encing some restlessness. The family needed a break. They had
taken turns sitting at her bedside, comforting her if she became
conscious, touching her arm, holding her hand, talking to her
softly. But over time, even the most dedicated, loving, family
needs time for routine, fun, laughter . . . normalcy.

When I saw the e-mail, my first instinct was to pretend it
wasn't there. Someone else would answer – someone who knew
what they were doing. I was certain that this family would want
someone with some experience sitting next to their mother, not
some scared new recruit. Of course, I was talking myself out
of it precisely *because* I was scared, and just as soon as I came to

that realization, I found myself responding to the e-mail. The response was simple: When do you need me?

There was still part of me that was hoping the shifts had been taken and that simply volunteering to go would somehow be enough. But those thoughts were quickly dispelled with a reply that came moments later. I would find myself walking to the car a few hours later on a chilly fall evening. I was set to relieve the previous volunteer at 11:00 PM, and I would remain bedside until 1:00 AM - a two-hour vigil. This would be my first experience, and I would go alone.

I remember my feelings very distinctly. "Nervous" certainly fits the bill, but this was different than walking on stage, speaking in front of a crowd, or getting ready to take a test. I just didn't know if I was *really* ready for this. I had trained for it, yes, but anyone can *train* for *anything*. I had arrived at this point in my life *because of a dog - A DOG*. I began to chuckle as I considered it. People must have thought I was nuts. This is what I have chosen to do with my free time - *This*. My doubt was driving the bus.

I didn't seem to be controlling my legs for some reason. They just walked toward the door. My brain was that little kid hiding behind the adult as we walked down the hallway to the room. My heart was racing, and I felt like throwing up. I also felt like bawling. *Keep it together . . . remember . . . you were called to do this*. Pushing me forward was the thought of how ridiculous it would have been to go through the emotionally-challenging training just to sit at home. Never had I trained for a half-marathon only to sit on the sidelines the morning of the race.

I turned the corner and stood in the doorway of the room, where a nurse was standing bedside. She saw me, and she did not look away. I will never forget that moment. She was looking at a terrified 44-year-old man who was about to bolt at any given second, and she knew it. She stopped what she was doing. Her eyes yielded, and her head was tilted slightly as she walked toward me with a gentle smile. I could see the client in the bed to the right. I didn't know if I could just look. Did I need to say something? Did I need to walk somewhere? I just didn't know. So I just stood there - immobile.

The nurse got to me, reached for my hand, and said simply, "All you have to do is make sure she is safe."

Everything became calm. My heart stopped racing. The little boy came out from behind the adult. My doubts washed away, and I had every sense that I was exactly where I was supposed to be. All because this angel, this incredible person I met for the very first time in that room on that evening, knew *exactly* what to say at the *exact* moment I needed to hear it. She spoke from years of compassionate care. She spoke from her heart.

In that moment, she calmed my "do not knows".

LEARNING TO DANCE

DANCE PARTNERS

Their steps don't match
The music
The sway they offer
Is their own

The love and adoration
For one another
Is felt by others
As they witness

They are in their
Own world
Dancing to music
Sixty-five years old

The first dance
Was shared
The night before
Distant shores called him away

But four minutes
Was sustenance enough
For three years
Of separation

A love – now decades old
Continually
Renewing
With every step

The music is no longer
Necessary
The dance floor
Is wherever they are

We can each feel love
But this
Is what
It looks like

Teach
Me
To
Dance

Somehow, we started talking about dancing. I recounted how my brother and I were not given a choice in the matter.

"When I was in junior high, my folks told me that it was time I learned how to dance," I told her. And that was that. Every Sunday afternoon for the next eight Sundays, my brother and I were carted off to learn ballroom dancing.

"This wasn't such a bad deal for my brother," I added, "he was dating someone, and it was a great excuse to get close to her."

Since I didn't have a date, my mom said she would fill the dance card. "The next time dance lessons rolled around, I made sure I had a date." Maggie laughed and laughed.

"We used to dance every week at the Pla-Mor," she said. I asked her if that's how she met her husband.

"No," she said, half smiling, half scowling. "We did lots of things together, but he didn't dance. Whenever I asked him to go dancing with us, he said he didn't know how and didn't care to learn." She emphasized her consternation by jabbing the air with her index finger.

"You were married a long time, Maggie – did you just go to the dances without him all those years, or did you just stop danc-ing?" I heard a slightly off-putting tone in my question as I con-sidered a sacrifice so great. She told me that during the course of their courtship, he had asked her to marry him at least half a dozen times, to which her reply was always very simply, "no."

Until after one rejection, he finally asked her why.

"I told him I wasn't going to marry someone who couldn't dance." Maggie paused, looked at his picture, and said with a smile,

"He learned."

BUCKLEY IN THE LEAD

MY EYES SPEAK

My voice
Is different
Than
Yours

Words
Spoken
Are
Long gone

But silence
Has
No
Hold

Look
At
My
Eyes

If you
Look away
You will
Not hear

You have
My
Permission
To stare

I
Need
To
Talk

I
Need
To be
Heard

I
Need
You to
Listen

Very quickly in our volunteering journey, we learned that when you meet one person with a terminal illness, you have met *one* person with a terminal illness. While the effects of a terminal illness are similar in the way it ravages the body, the journey itself is intensely personal and individual-specific. The amount of time we have to spend with a person on this journey can vary greatly; our visits have ranged from one week to many months. In some cases, clients will "graduate" hospice care, meaning the illness has either stopped progressing or slowed enough that hospice care is no longer warranted. We experienced one such client, and while we were certainly happy for her, it also meant that our visits ended. Our final visit with her was bittersweet.

Buckley and I begin our client relationships with him in the lead. I wish I could include a video of how this plays out time and time again. As soon as he enters the room, there is a celebration of sorts. There is sincere appreciation and gratitude for this beautiful dog who has come to see "me". He is never shy. Once he sniffs out the room, his approach is always the same. He walks to the client, sits beside the chair, and stays. As long as a hand is on him, he doesn't move. He does this not because of any training I was able to accomplish. He learned this on his own, and it is magical to watch.

I saw Betty in the dayroom during one of our scheduled visits to another client in the same building. At the time, Betty was not one of our clients, so we did not visit her. Over the course of our first year of volunteering, we learned that Buckley had limits on how much time and how many people he could serve before he needed a break. Initially, we would visit our clients, but soon after we arrived on campus, requests for his presence would come.

Our visits would then extend to other individual rooms, lunch rooms, day rooms and other places where people had gathered – hospice and non-hospice. Before we knew it, we would be circulating for 3-4 hours, and I would see Buckley begin to lose focus. Additionally, when we would get home, he would immediately retreat to the deck and in his own way, request no visitors while he replenished. For Buckley's well-being, we had to impose some limitations, and we discovered the magic number was no more than four clients per week. One of the toughest things I have had to learn how to do in this line of volunteering is to gently decline when asked if we could stop for a visit.

When the time came to introduce another client to Buckley, I inquired about Betty. I wanted to know if she liked dogs and if she would like visits from Buckley. Betty had severe limitations, and while hospice volunteers are provided with medical information that details specific illnesses, I don't remember hers. In fact, it has never been a focus for us. I read the information, but my focus has always zeroed in on making sure I understood any limitations. I want to know any topics that they liked or didn't like and any other information that would be important for me to know during our initial visits. After that, it was easy to let things develop organically.

Betty's arms were bent upward and her hands curled in, she was confined to either a bed or wheelchair, and she could not communicate vocally other than making non-specific sounds. She had to be tilted back in her chair so she would not fall out. Most tragically, she was fully aware of her surroundings and had no cognitive limitations. She was trapped inside her own body. But, she loved dogs, and that was all that mattered to us.

Betty communicated with her eyes. We would ask yes or no questions, and she would blink once or twice depending on the answer. She was also very emotional, and tears would frequently fall - often out of frustration, but mostly because of her circumstances. Very quickly we learned that her answers were in her eyes, as was her connection to the world. While Buckley sat near where Betty could see him, we simply sat with her – sometimes in conversation, other times quietly.

As time passed, we would ask the same questions initially: Are you eating? Are you sleeping? Are you in any pain? Is anything different today? Week after week, Betty answered those four questions by blinking "yes", "yes", "no", "no", respectively. Then one day she answered "yes" to the last question, followed by tears. I knew what that meant, and I just held her hand and cried with her.

MORE TIME

MEMORIAL DAY

It is indeed right
To dedicate
A day
To those who have
Left their shells behind

I am humbled
As I stand
And am applauded
For the service I have performed
For my country

In church
At band stands
In prayer meetings
At banquets
At concerts

My humility is born
From the service and sacrifice
Of those who
Have served and have given
The Last Full Measure

And I am often
Taken to my knees by the tears
In an old man's blue eyes

As he recounts the horror
Of serving in action

The tears magnify the burden on his soul
The images
Remain
Unblemished
By time

A young man hell-bent on
Glory
Became an old man
With the first pull
Of the trigger

We continually re-create
Ninety-year-old twenty-somethings
Because we don't listen
To the old man
Whose tears tell a story

We remember those
Who have left their
Burdens behind
And those who
Still carry them

Our visit began as it had for many months before.

In my experience, terminal illnesses move at their own speed, with little or no control exercised by its host. With Eleanor, her illness had been merciful, and she had continued to live pain-free and remain active. Experience has also taught me that every second is one to cherish, as mercy is not endless.

"Are you eating okay?" I asked.

"Yes." This rarely changed.

"Are you sleeping well?"

"Never have any problem sleeping," she said, which is usually followed by a laugh.

"Are you getting your exercise?" She takes 20 laps up and down the hallway every day. She never misses a day.

"Got my laps in early today," she smiled.

"Are you in any pain?" Eleanor just rolls with the questions as I ask them. She knows they are coming.

"Nope." She had chronic pain in her right shoulder, but she knew it would never resolve. All this while she loves on Buckley. "Sweetie" is her name for him.

"How are you today, Sweetie?" Buckley looks directly at her, sitting, attentive. He is an amazing dog.

This day was Memorial Day, which is different than Veteran's Day. On this day, we take time to reflect upon those who have served and have now passed away. For me, it is more solemn than Veteran's Day, where we take time to honor all who have served – those who have passed away, and those who are still living. On Veteran's Day, we still have an opportunity to lay our hands on someone who understands better than most the honor of service and the sacrifice necessary to fulfill that service. On Memorial Day, we have only the memories of those loved ones.

"It's Memorial Day today, Eleanor," I said.

"Yes, it is." There was a pause. "I suppose they'll probably have a flag on my son's gravesite."

We had spoken together every Monday for months, and she had never mentioned her son's death. Her eyes had tears in them. I gently reached for her hand – the hand that wasn't petting Buckley – and I was already glassy-eyed as we both sat for a moment not talking.

"Eleanor . . . I am so sorry for your loss. I didn't know you had a son who served. I wish I could have met him." I sat with her, both of us crying. I know the sadness that comes with losing a brother, and as deep as that sadness goes, the grief of losing a child is a bottomless well. I watched as Buckley moved in a little closer to her. She noticed him doing so, and she hugged him.

"God gave you something special in this dog," she said.

"I know. He also didn't hold back on the mischief." It is sometimes difficult to keep your composure at times like this. I have come to use humor. I have found that it allows the conversation to continue uninhibited.

"My son died of cancer 12 years ago," she went on, "seems like yesterday. It still hurts so much. He was such a good man. He served a tour in Vietnam during the thick of it.

"I just wanted more time," she said, after a pause.

I told her about one of my first hospice clients . . . the shared story about the meaning of time, the seconds on the clock, and the importance of using them. Eleanor looked at her clock, ticking away.

"I hope you know how precious this life is and the time you have to live it," she said, speaking to me, but looking at Buckley.

She talked about her son a little more, and the stories included laughter amid the pain. Slowly, the conversation moved to different subjects, and I followed her lead, with the understanding that what had been spoken was all that would be shared. I left her as I always do – gently grasping her hand, telling her that she would be in my thoughts all week until next Monday.

I also thanked her son for his service, and I thanked her for her sacrifice. In honor of Eleanor, her son and all families who understand service and sacrifice, I dedicate this poem. It is the only poem I have written with five-line stanzas.

TO LAUGH IS TO LIVE

GOD TAUGHT ME

My turn
To write
What I know
About God

An ice cold beer
After working hard all day
Outside on the berm
Satisfaction

The adoption of one son
The birth of another
Taken to my knees with emotion
Love

The death of a brother
Who two weeks prior
Was dancing the fox-trot
Suffering

New love
Food and sleep optional
Irrepressible energy
Passion

Dropping everything
To listen
To help shoulder the burden
Compassion

The comedian
A gin-like dry wit
An infectious smile
Laughter

Skinned knees
And disappointment
Lending you a hand to get back up
Encouragement

A pew
Taught
Me
Fear

God
Taught
Me
The rest

It wasn't going to be a routine visit.

Everything else was routine – Buckley brushing and primp-ing, a little pep talk, brushing his mate Cooper (which was al-ways necessary, as he was consistently jealous of whatever I was doing with Buckley at any moment of the day), donning the vest, and off we went. For the past couple months, our first visit of the day had been with Roger, and we had come to expect the same enthusiastic greeting: "How ya doin', Buckley ol' Buddy?!"

On this Monday, Roger was clearly agitated. When he spoke, the source of his agitation was clear, as he was suddenly tooth-less. Whether his dentures were misplaced or accidentally dis-carded was unclear, but the fact was that now he had to cope – at least temporarily – with puréed meals. For anyone, this would not be a fun proposition. For someone who is actively dying, it's a real kick in the pants.

He explained that he would have to endure this situation for ten days while new dentures were fitted and obtained. That day, Buckley and I got to hear the cussing of an actual WW II sailor. Buckley and I were both impressed. And I grew up on a farm.

I knew with time, Roger's emotions would calm and his humor would return, so Buckley and I put a plan in motion. We decided that we wanted Roger to be prepared should he ever be in need of temporary replacement dentures again. Therefore, we ventured out to costume shops and gag gift stores throughout the city to find the perfect variety of "tem-porary replacements" (in the form of goblin teeth, vampire teeth, a set with a missing tooth or two, and a beautiful set with some diamond and ruby bling). We then waited for the perfect time to present them to him.

Two weeks later, we found our opportunity. When we entered the room, Roger was his old self and in very good spirits. He was up and about and getting ready to go on a walk. We approached him in a very serious tone, and I told him that Buckley and I took it upon ourselves to purchase a set of replacements in case another unfortunate incident like this should befall him again.

"You did?" he said, a bit taken back, "you really didn't need to do that!" I didn't say anything. I simply presented a beautiful, sparkling blue box with a ribbon on it.

Roger took the box from my hands, and when he opened the box, a fit of laughter ensued. It was the kind of genuine, pain-in-the-side laughter that comes so rarely, but is so necessary. He tried on every piece, and every time he looked in the mirror, the laughter began again. We must have laughed for half an hour. When we thought we were done laughing, he would put the vampire teeth on again and speak with a Dracula voice, and it would all start again.

Roger passed away just two weeks later. When Buckley and I went to the memorial service, his wife came to us with a sparkly blue box with a ribbon tied around it and a smile on her face.

"Roger said that he wouldn't need these where he was going. He wanted to make sure I gave them to you," she said.

She pulled me away from the other people who were there, and went on to recommend with a chuckle that I give them a good rinsing out.

I'm sure the others were wondering just what was so funny, but I figured if she was laughing, I could too.

"God Taught Me" was written not only with Roger and our hospice clients in mind but also how my time with them has affected my own philosophy. I spent my entire childhood and young adult life learning about a God who I was taught to "fear and love". My own personal struggle began when I experienced the birth of my son. As I looked at this newborn baby and immediately fell head-over-heals in love, I pondered how it could be that my God could ever vanquish him to everlasting damnation for something he did – or even *could* do – simply because he was a "flawed" human being. In an instant, the concept of original sin was garbled as was the concept of hell. Neither one of them made sense to me anymore.

My sudden raging cognitive dissonance was especially untimely as, at the time, I was working at a church. I could no longer teach the concepts in which I did not believe, and yet I needed a way to support my family (fortunately, I was able to transition into full-time military service). While this internal struggle was playing out, I also felt an incredible weight lifted off my shoulders. It was as if God Himself was welcoming me into the light of awakeness – *finally* realizing that love really is the only thing.

This puzzles people. I am asked, if there is no hell, how do people keep from doing bad things? I get it. The thought process is that there *has* to be some form of punishment, otherwise people will default to running amok without fear of consequence. But I have found the opposite to be true. Once the fear of some kind of "hell" was removed, I no longer had to look at God as someone to be afraid of, but only as a force that partnered for acts of love, kindness, compassion and grace.

And yet, it is a difficult concept for many, and I get it. These are my beliefs only, and I arrived at where I am because of the *struggle* on which I embarked to discover these beliefs. There are no easy answers – that's why it's called a struggle. There are still bad people in the world doing bad things. From time to time, we all do bad things. But in the end, if my own sons did something so horrific and were languishing away in prison awaiting a death sentence, I would still be there for them. I would never want to be separated from them, because I am their father and I love them. Nothing that they do could ever separate that love from them. And if I feel that way about my children, just think of the love God has for me.

In the same way, I don't think God takes us from our loved ones because he needs them back, or has another plan. I don't believe God planned to take my brother from me, his parents, his other siblings, his wife, his two-year-old daughter, or his friends. Instead, he was there, in that ditch after the car accident, holding him and feeling the pain only a parent can feel at the loss of a child. And He feels that pain with all of us today.

Over the years serving hospice clients, I have held the hands of the agnostic, the atheist, and the Christian. All of them have lived their own personal struggles, and none of them were different in their compassion, grace and love.

They would all tell you that these are the only things that matter.

COURAGE

TEN SECONDS OF COURAGE

I had the words
But I
Did not
Speak

I was paralyzed
And yet
I was
Standing

What
Might have been
Was now
Gone

A Memory
Of my imagination
Known only
To me

Ten
Seconds
Of
Courage

To speak
To move
To act
To inspire

Throwing
Caution
To the
Wind

To
Defend
A
Stranger

To give
Voice
To
Your heart

Heather is not a hospice client. She is my wife, and the universe encouraged her to take a chance; my hospice clients have taught me to have the courage to pay attention.

Heather and I have known each other for years, as our families lived just down the street from each other. But as my marriage ended and I moved to a different neighborhood, friendships that had been made while married had either ended or become distant, as often happens during something as intensely personal as divorce. While our children were close growing up, our families were not particularly close. This was mainly because Heather's kids were involved in about every kind of activity in the city, and she spent her life bouncing between them. When I moved, I didn't expect to see her again.

I spent the next seven years learning how to be single while I mourned the loss of a marriage and focused on raising my kids. I dated, and even thought I may have found another person with whom I could spend the rest of my life until that fell apart. I dated again, but as soon as anything had the least little hint of anything serious, I would get scared, push back, or run away. I decided that I was going to remain single for the rest of my life. It would be my dogs and me, and we would be just fine.

Done.

And then lightning struck from a clear blue sky. Not coincidentally, it happened on Monday, September 12, 2016, and just as Buckley and I were on our way home after our hospice visits for the day (Hallmark could not write this stuff). My phone alerted me to a message, and it was from Heather. We reconnected in April of that same year while she was attending an event at which I was speaking. She came up to me afterwards and asked if I remembered her. She was hardly someone you could forget. We had a very brief conversation (about what, I can't recall – but I know "status" was not discussed), we became Facebook friends, and that was that. I didn't really expect to hear from her again.

The message on September 12 said simply, "Hey Stuart, how are you these days?". While it would take more conversation to discover that both of us were single, I became that kid who does a cannonball into the pool. No caution, no testing. All in. My previous commitment to "single-hood" was vanquished. I became a guy who would tell himself to "not screw this up" with every text or interaction that would follow.

I was in love.

I would discover later that she was encouraged to reach out to me by her son, Heath. She had confided in him that she would like to talk to me. Still, she was unsure if I would even answer. In his own way, Heath told her not to waste any time and summon ten seconds of courage to send me a note.

I am forever indebted to him for fortifying her courage. It left me with this poem, *Ten Seconds of Courage*. It speaks to the openness of love but also to any action necessary to not only find the courage but to act upon it. One simple act of grace, kindness or compassion can – and does – change the trajectory of what *might have been* into what *is*. And most often, it is the very little thing that, when acted upon, changes the world.

BUCKLEY AND THE LITTLE GIRL

IT'S THE ROUTINE days that sneak up and grab you.

This was going to be a regular Monday morning. We would stop first to visit Agnes who is not under hospice care. We stopped in to see her a year and a half ago on the way to see one of our scheduled clients. Since then, we have been starting our Mondays the same way. She is 92 years old and going strong.

We would then be off to visit Dorothy who is one of our scheduled hospice clients and resides in a building next door. Rarely do we visit her in her room. She is always in the middle of her workout routine when we arrive. She moves her wheelchair along with her feet up and down the hallway five times in the morning and again in the afternoon. We caught her doing the same today.

Only this time she motioned for us to come to her instead of the regular routine of waiting for her to come to us so as not to interrupt her exercise. She was about halfway down the hallway, and when we got to where she was, we noticed that there was a lot of luggage and assorted bags outside one of the rooms. Dorothy explained to us that the resident in that room was declining quickly; the bags were from all of the family members who had traveled to be at her bedside for her final hours.

"There's a little girl in that room," Dorothy said, "I know how much Buckley loves kids. Maybe if we sit here for a bit, that little girl might come out to pet Buckley."

Dorothy had an endless supply of grace and kindness. I agreed it was the perfect place to sit and visit.

As happens frequently, word travels very quickly when there is a dog in the building – especially when he locks eyes with you. The little girl was hesitant until Buckley encouraged her with a wag of his tail. As she walked toward us, Dorothy took the lead.

"Do you like dogs?" she said as the little girl nodded. "This is Buckley. You can give him hugs and squeezes." I chuckled as Dorothy suddenly somehow became Buckley's master. I sat back and watched the magic happen. Her name was Emily, and she was five years old.

"Are you here visiting?" Dorothy asked. Again, Emily nodded as she stood face-to-face with Buckley, petting him. Dorothy knew Emily was here visiting her grandmother, and she also knew that seeing her grandmother unconscious was scary for her. We continued to pet Buckley until Emily spoke.

"My gramma is in that room," she paused, "we are all waiting for her to . . . ". Emily then pointed upward. She then began to cry, and she naturally hugged Buckley as her head turned sideways on his neck and shoulders, his fur absorbing her tears.

When a kid cries, adults cry. We all sat there for at least another twenty minutes, mostly talking to Buckley. Finally, Emily was ready to go back into the room.

As Dorothy and I said our goodbyes, we watched Emily walk back to her family. I walked slowly beside Dorothy as she moved her wheelchair back to her room. "You are a real sweetheart, Dorothy. You are just nothing but pure love," I said.

She looked at me, took my hand and squeezed, but she didn't speak. Facing her own mortality with a realism that can only be felt by others of the same, I wondered if she was thinking with an increased awareness of her own very limited time.

But I know Dorothy. She was only thinking of that little girl.

AGNES

WITH MANY YEARS of hospice volunteering under my belt, I have been somewhat conditioned to feel an immediate twinge of sadness when the phone rings with a number I don't recognize.

"Stuart? This is Julie, Agnes' daughter. Are you and Buckley still planning on visiting mom today?"

We had been visiting Agnes for about a year and a half, and our visits began quite by coincidence. She was never an assigned client of Buckley's. She saw us walk through the building on the way to an assigned client, and she asked if she could pet him. Every week since, it's the way Buckley and I began our Monday mornings.

Her health changed rapidly after she fell and broke her hip. When she felt up for a visit, we stopped in to see her, but it was clear that she knew her time was limited.

Somehow to me, Agnes was infallible. Week after week, she was the same – always slept well, always ate well, and always knew and cared for the other residents. She talked of her family often, and she shared the most wonderful stories about her husband

and life growing up. We became close. I wasn't there to check up on her. I was there visiting a friend.

"Yes. We will be there. Has there been a change?" I asked.

"Yes, there has," Julie informed, "she has been actively dying since Friday. But everyone has said their goodbyes, and yet she is still holding on. We think she may be waiting for Buckley to come for one last visit. Do you think that might be possible?"

"I think that is very possible," I said. "We will be there shortly."

I used to attempt to compartmentalize emotion while visiting hospice clients, but I discovered this was just silly. The simple truth is that you just can't help but to connect, and the connection is an emotional investment with a full awareness that one day very soon you will have to say goodbye. With every connection I have made, I have experienced grace, compassion, kindness and love – none of which would have been possible had I pretended to be holding hands with a painting.

When we got there, Buckley ran into the room, but things were different. Agnes wasn't in her chair. Instead, we sat at her bedside. I took her hand.

"Agnes – we are here. Buckley is right beside you. We are both happy to see you. Thank you for waiting for us." There was no stopping the tears this time.

We sat for some time. It was good to see Julie again. She explained to us that her mom had insisted that they remember to give Buckley the two Beanie Puppies that he always had to have in his mouth as they visited.

"You should feel very proud – I didn't even make the list!" Julie said, laughing through her tears.

When we prepared to leave, we took the Beanie Puppies, we hugged each family member, and then I turned to Agnes and held her hand once again.

"Agnes – thank you for waiting for us." I had a difficult time letting go of her hand.

It would be a day that Buckley would provide just as much comfort to me as he does for so many others.

BEAUTIFUL BOY

THERE ARE TIMES when our visits with our clients are shorter than usual. Another appointment may have them occupied. Such was the case on this Monday morning.

With some extra time on our hands, Buckley and I went to the main building to wander the hallways. As we walked, we came upon sounds of distress coming from a room. It was only later that I discovered the resident, Gracie, had just received her diagnosis, and she was very upset. As we approached, I heard the social worker tell her that she saw a dog coming down the hallway and wondered if she would like a visit.

"NO!" she yelled. "Don't even think of bringing that dog in this room! You are only trying to distract me!" No words that were coming from the social worker or Gracie's husband would bring any comfort.

Gracie's physical condition left her severely bent in her wheelchair; she could not see us, and we did not make a sound. Buckley just sat at my side. The social worker motioned for us to wait down the hallway but not to leave, so we repositioned ourselves and waited. Gracie continued to resist any attempts of comfort. Finally, out of sheer exhaustion, she fell asleep. Her husband stayed with her as the social worker came to us and told us a little more about Gracie.

"Gracie loves dogs," she assured me, "We really thought it would help." She went on to apologize.

"There is no need to apologize," I reassured, as Buckley seemed to agree with every wag of his tail. We talked for a few more minutes, and I learned more about Gracie. For her entire life, she had always had dogs, but we couldn't force a relationship with Buckley. As we visited, I had an idea.

"What would you think about Buckley and I making another stop next week, but this time, we will just sit in the lobby," I explained. "Then, if Gracie is up for a stroll, maybe you could bring her by." The idea was to have Gracie come upon us by accident, however planned that accident was. We both agreed it was worth a shot, but it would take some acting on everyone's part.

The day came, and we did as we had planned, and we waited in the lobby. Gracie's husband was in on the plan, and I saw him coming toward us with her. She was bent over and could not see us. The social worker watched from a distance.

When they got close enough, Gracie's husband spoke. "Gracie, there's a dog in front of you. Would you like to see him?" Gracie immediately turned to see Buckley and sat up straighter than she had in days.

"Oh aren't you a beautiful boy," she went on, "you are so pretty. Oh, and so soft!" This went on for a period of time, and her conversation with Buckley never stopped. I hadn't noticed that the social worker had joined us. She was smiling.

I looked up at Gracie's husband, standing behind the wheelchair with his hands on the handles, watching. He had tears streaming down his cheeks. It was a moment he had hoped for – a moment of peace and calm and love in the midst of an incredibly difficult situation.

Eventually, Gracie became tired, and though she could no longer stay, she didn't want to leave.

"Thank you, Buckley. You are such a beautiful boy. Thank you." She went back to her room. Buckley and I retreated to a private area.because I knew I couldn't hold back the tears. I hugged him and told him all of the things I heard Gracie tell him.

Although Gracie had just received her prognosis, she passed away only two weeks later. We only had one visit, but one I will never forget.

STANDARD QUESTIONS, CHANGING ANSWERS

SNOWFALL

I have
Never
Had
Cancer

But I watched
The snowfall
As if I
Had survived it

I hugged
My child
As if I
Had just been diagnosed

I watched
An
Entire
Sunset

I smelled a glass
Of wine
More than
I drank it

I Listened to
The words of a friend
As if they were
The last I would ever hear

I noticed
The second hand
On my clock
For the first time

Every kiss
Became one
To
Remember

The snowfall
Was
The most beautiful
I had ever seen.

FALL

Hello Friend
I've
Missed
You

Your crisp
Kiss
Of the cool
Morning air

The tilt of the earth
Finally working
In our
Favor

Please unpack
And
Stay
A while

Enjoy with me
That bottle of red
Held back
For your arrival

Sit with me
And take in
The beautiful paintings
You are about to create

Anticipate with me
The incense
Cut grass, campfires
Pumpkin spice

And the first
Firing
Of the
Furnace

Celebrate with me
Your many holidays
And the love
Of friends and family

Your glass is
Empty
Have
Another

"Have you been eating okay?"

"Have you been getting your sleep?"

"Are you in any pain?"

These are the standard questions I ask of any hospice client Buckley and I serve. The questions usually come after some initial visiting and after Buckley has brought smiles and comfort. It becomes routine, and for Olivia, the questions always revealed that she had been eating fine, sleeping well, and living without pain.

Buckley and I become attached to all of our clients. Their stories bring perspective and warmth, sorrow, and humor. But mostly the attachment originates from the way in which our clients teach us how to live.

For Olivia, her heart sang in anyone who met her. It was difficult to understand her at first; she was limited in her ability to speak. But after a while, we knew her words. Her physical limitations didn't allow her to fully express the love she had for Buckley and all those people who loved her. We just moved Buckley in closer so the back of her hand could feel the soft fur. Buckley always obliged with some licks.

I am not opposed to Buckley's licking. But sometimes, Buckley licks…and licks, and licks, and LICKS. Where I might normally encourage Buckley to manifest his love sans the slobber, Olivia delighted in the "washing" of her hands. I was gently admonished if I tried to stop him.

A few weeks ago, when I asked Olivia the standard questions, she cried. She could tell something was different. Something was changing. She knew what was happening. These moments are unforgettable in any circumstance with every client, but this moment was different somehow. All I could do was hold her hand and cry with her. I knew what the tears meant. I knew how much Olivia loved to live life, and she was not ready to say goodbye. Her body was controlling that destiny – now at a quickened pace.

The last week, when Olivia was confined to her bed, I witnessed humanity and compassion that could only come from those destined to a similar fate. Residents of the same facility, all of whom had a terminal illness themselves, made their way to Olivia's room. They touched her face, held her hand, kissed her forehead...and sang to her. Comfort from those who will one day need the same comfort.

At Olivia's memorial service, Buckley and I followed our normal routine but not on our normal day. Those days are never normal days. He was brushed, his vest buckled, and I talked to him as I always do. "You are needed," I said. "Today, we will meet Olivia's family and friends."

His stare was a familiar one to me of course. It is unchanging, constant, and devoted. Just as he provides a level of comfort to loved ones, he carries me.

The poems "Snowfall" and "Fall" are dedicated to Olivia. She was a painter. She used her mouth to hold a paintbrush, and an assistant would mix the paint and arrange the canvas. At her memorial service (which Buckley and I always try to attend), we were presented with one of her paintings that now hangs in my office. As I read these poems, I imagine the beautiful paintings, and I remember Olivia.

THE CROWDED EMPTY SPACE

THE CROWDED EMPTY SPACE

The table
Was oversized
For just
One person

One chair
Waiting
Sturdy, but
Alone

Six
Hours
Of
Interrogation

The eyes
Of
The
Questioners

Saw one
Man
One
Table

Standing
Unseen
At my side
Behind me

My mom
My dad
My brothers, sister
My teachers, friends

My confidantes
My mentors
My failures
My successes

Never once
Did I
Feel
Alone

In the
Crowded
Empty
Space

The entirety of the interview was six hours. It consisted of three separate interviews with a board of community residents, faculty and the school board itself. Each had their own set of questions. I had prepared well, but it was clear that an interview for a superintendent of public schools was going to be unlike any interview I had ever had before. In total, there were four candidates out of a field of twenty-six applications. I felt fortunate that I made the cut, especially since this was my first application for a superintendency.

I was the outsider. While I had teaching experience, I was currently in the military. During my service, I made a conscious effort to stay connected to education not only with my continuing educational path, but also with the partnership I had formed with a small, rural public school in Nebraska. I attended school board meetings on a monthly basis for years, and I formed solid relationships with both the principal and superintendent, both of whom I consider friends and mentors to this day. On my journey, I had applied for countless principal positions, but I was rejected by literally every school district. I received a handful of interviews, but I got the feeling that they were mostly offered out of pity.

It became clear to me that the position on which I should be focusing was the *district* leadership position and not the building leadership position. This is why I began working on my doctorate degree. Still, my shot at such a prestigious (although most superintendents might argue against such a descriptor) position was very slim as the outsider. I was not going to be unprepared for such an opportunity when it did present itself.

I studied the community. I poured over the tax information. I visited with residents over lunch at a local gas station (it also had the only restaurant). I reviewed the budget with state officials. There wasn't a thing I had not looked at, studied, or observed. I knew the price of corn, the beef market, and the land values over the course of the last twenty years. I was ready.

And I rocked the interview. I was comfortable. I was relaxed. I was confident but genuinely humble. And by the end of the six hours, I was absolutely spent. But I was also overjoyed, and I immediately called my sister to share my feelings.

"I left it all out on the field," I said, almost with tears in my eyes. My sister was celebrating with me, as I explained the entire evening. She clung to every word, listening intently as if there was a surprise at the end of every sentence. Of all the people in the world, she knew better than most what it meant to strive for something you love, and there was no one else I would have wanted to talk to at that moment.

I received the phone call the next morning: I didn't get the job. While I was disappointed, I still felt a calm satisfaction that I had done all I could do.

This poem was written after some reflection on the experience, but "disappointment" never really entered the writing process. Of course the feelings were there - the preparation, the research, the *time* spent focusing intensely on such a venture . . . only to have *nothing to show for it*. Some said there was benefit in having the interview experience, and while that does hold merit, no one likes hearing it.

But the poem focuses on something I said during the interview. I told the board that while they saw just one person sitting in front of them, what they didn't see was the crowded empty space behind me.

It is within that crowded empty space that my resiliency resides. In failure, there is still inspiration. With such a crowded empty space, there is no struggle that does not have an answer. There isn't a mistake that hasn't been made and forgiveness given. Self-doubt is countered with patience and reassurance. Overconfidence is met with humility. If I feel knocked down, worn out, or frustrated, there isn't someone who hasn't already shown me how to get back up, restore, or refocus. And while the pain I feel in any situation is unique to me, it has already been felt by others. There is always comfort and understanding. In any empty space I reside, there is a crowd beckoning me onward.

Never once have I felt alone in my crowded, empty, space.

THE SIGN

CLOSED

The sign
Was met
With
Disappointment

As I once again
Missed my chance
To get
What I needed

That I must
Wait again for the sign
To change
As I know it will

I chuckled as I
Pondered the idea
Of wearing
A sign

An unmistakable
Indication
For all
To see

"Open"
Or
"Closed"
It would read

"Closed" may be
Met
With
Disappointment

But just wait
For the sign
To
Change

I
Know
It
Will

HOPE

The
Source
Of
Sleepless nights

And the
Source
Of
Survival

It
Does
Spring
Eternal

But
Sometimes
I
Wish

It would
Just
Go
Away

And just let
An
Idea
Die

Or just let
A
Relationship
End

Instead
It holds
A loving
Embrace

Forever
A partner
To
Resiliency

And
A spark
To
Our dreams

On sort of a whim (again, the universe comes in to play), I embarked on a solo road trip to Punxsutawney, PA on January 31, 2010 – yes, to see Punxsutawney Phil. While I do love local traditions (although this is more of an international tradition), this trip had more to do with me just getting away. The total windshield time from my house was a little over twenty hours, and my destination was a little cabin in the middle of a heavily wooded campground – with no cell phone service.

I had only recently been divorced. Divorce is a lifelong journey of pain and healing - where you end up is sort of like how you begin again after the death of a loved one (which I also experienced with my brother's tragic death in 2001). You emerge as yourself, 2.0. You are the same you, but you are different in sometimes subtle, sometimes profound ways. And as we have discovered with cell phone upgrades, you are never really "fixed". Divorce and death aren't things you "get over". They are things that are added to who you are and how you walk this earth. They are new starting points. When you experience such powerful events, everything changes. The sunrise is different, the smell of coffee, relationships, people . . . nothing is the same or ever will be. This took me some time to understand. To some degree, I am still understanding it.

When I finally did comprehend what this change meant, the burden was lifted because I knew that I didn't need to get back to *who I was* – which would have ultimately been impossible and defeatist. Instead, I could begin living life as *who I am now* and *who I am becoming.* For me, this continues to mean lots of patience, reflection, and forgiveness. I didn't know it then, but the road trip to Punxsutawney was forty hours of windshield time that offered a beginning of a journey on which I still travel today.

"Closed" came directly from that trip. As I was driving along the countryside near the remote campground, I came upon a small shop that had a cute homemade sign that read, very plainly, "Closed for the Winter".

"That's a long time," I thought to myself.

That started a thought process. How nice it would be if we could all just wear a sign like this from time to time. Not forever, mind you – just enough for us to take some necessary time for reflection and understanding. The sign would be clear enough for others to give us some space without an explanation as to why. As the poem indicates, the sign will change. Just give it some time.

Then, there is "Hope" – a perfect partner to "Closed". As the poem indicates, hope is a dichotomy of sorts. The sleepless nights are the result of both excitement and fear and how much easier life would sometimes be if an idea would just go away and leave us alone. In the end, however, it is what drives us and pushes us to pursue whatever it is that the universe has in store.

THE BEGINNING

OUR JOURNEY CONTINUES. This book, while an encapsulation of transformative experiences, is a starting point. I have shared how a cold, wet, nose has led me to an understanding and enlightenment that began as a gentle nudge but has now developed into a constant driving force, continually beckoning me on. The closest I have come to describing the feeling has been to label it as an affliction, but without the pain and suffering. There is always a "next" thing. There is always something to attach to my seconds.

The driving force is all-encompassing. It isn't a limited focus based solely on writing a book, building a college, or finishing a doctorate. It is the force behind continually striving to become a better dad, a more gracious husband, a more involved community member, and a more loving son and brother. It has meant committing to sacrificing for the better good for which I have admittedly not always been successful.

As I write these sentences, I am a person committing to the unknown with the faith that potential is nothing if it is not to be fulfilled. I have been here before with different unknowns in front of me, but I have always turned back. But the uncomfortable, beautiful unknown is a place inhabited by so few, with space mostly reserved for those who only intended to go, but didn't. I have held the hands of many people whose reservations were never met. They had it within themselves to uncover the potential that was within, but instead conformed to the traditional, the "normal". To label the path I have chosen as a leap of faith is cliché. It would be more apropos to call it a leap of terror. But to do differently would be to push all I have learned aside as if it had never happened. It would be to *know*, but not *do*.

Sharing what I have learned by *doing* becomes the driving force and manifests itself in discovering ways to incorporate this knowledge into action steps. Whether it is a book, a speaking engagement, or a college, the inception is the same. The same urgency resides within you regardless of where you are or what you are doing. The seconds I am using are the exact same seconds you are using – or *not* using, if that is the case. The only difference between an ordinary life and an extraordinary life is the way in which you use your seconds.

The call I have for you is to question how you are using them. A re-evaluation doesn't mean you will one day live in nirvana. It is simply a plea that is passed along from those who understand better than most the value of something the rest of us take for granted every day. The time you have is limited. Your seconds are finite. If you handed out seconds from a basket you carried around from day to day, and you witnessed your dwindling supply, would you reconsider the way in which they were distributed? And to whom? Would you continue to invest them in a job you hate, a relationship that is not based upon mutual respect, or potential that continues to go unfulfilled?

A job doesn't define you. A relationship doesn't define you. How you choose to use your seconds defines you, because using your seconds is completely within your control. Each second is a sacred gift given *from you* to some *thing*. Dying people want you to know that you simply do not have the luxury of casting them about without care. Buckley wants you to know that the seconds that have passed are not as important as the ones that are in front of you now.

What are you doing with them?

EPILOGUE

It is worth noting that I don't have a poem about Buckley. It has not been for a lack of trying. I have started and stopped at least a dozen times. I don't have an explanation.

Maybe he defies words. Maybe everything you have read *is* Buckley. There is a look of humility about him that appears to deflect any praise, but I am often brought back to reality when it appears he is actually *reacting* to the compliments and hamming it up. My family members see him as any other dog – loyal, dependable, faithful – always ready to accept a nugget from the popcorn bowl or a piece of bacon from the skillet, and always ready for a belly rub. But every Monday, I witness love that simply cannot be explained in a way that would do him justice.

We recently graduated what may end up being our final re-certification process which occurs every two years. By the end of this cycle (and if we are fortunate enough to live that long), Buckley will have given six and a half years of his very short life to the comfort and care of people in the final days, weeks, or months of their lives. This will equate to over half of his life. I can only imagine the heavenly preparations that are already taking place for him when it is his time.

For Buckley, this is just what he does, or what he has been called to do. I have merely authored his acts of grace, love, and compassion, so they can be shared. Just as I have told his story, I have shared some of mine, and the transformation of my life through the love of a cold, wet, nose.

But the transformation continues. For me, there is still much work to be done.

POEMS (IN ORDER OF APPEARANCE)

ONE SECOND

We
Hardly
Notice
Them

Unless
One
Is
Required

And there
Are no more
To be
Spared

That's how
It goes
You
See

That
Which
We
Have

Is that
Which we
Take
For granted

Enlightenment
Is
The
Cure

But it
Comes
At
A cost

We
Are
A silly
Lot

TIME

More prose
About time
A love-hate
Relationship

Too much
Never enough
If only I had more
When will it pass?

Always living in the present
Forever hopeful of the future
Saddened by regrets
Of the past.

Forgetful of it in the midst
Of love.
A prison sentence
At love's loss.

Captured in photographs
Alive in the
Hands
Of a clock

Represented by wrinkles
Rings of the Oak Tree
Shapes of the Moon
And the Promise of Spring

Mortal enemy
To those who
Have been cheated
By terminal illness

A gift
For those
Who have survived
It

Longing for more
When silence replaces words left unspoken
And death claims the life
Of a loved one

Just one
Second more
To say
I love you.

TIME II

You
Are
A tricky
Bastard

A
Disappearing act
At life's
End

An uninvited
Unwanted guest
During
Heartbreak

And
Yet
You
Heal

With the
Gift
Of
Years

And the
Subtle presence
Of a
Butterfly

Allowing
Love to
Spring eternal
Once again

You
Are
A tricky
Bastard

A CALLING

It is
A
Daunting
Task

For which
Most
Never
Accomplish

Some
Fail
To
Begin

Lacking the
Courage
To vanquish
The fear

And allow
The light
From
Within

To give
Permission for others
To do
The same

Who do
You suppose
You
Are?

What many things
Has the Universe
Assigned
To you?

On a
Silver platter
They
Exist

Patience
Awareness
Urgency
Indeed . . . urgency

For you
Were not
Created
Just for you

LITTLE VOICE

It is silent
But
It speaks
Volumes

It is ever-present
And points
True
North

It has
The patience
Of
Job

And the
Urgency
Of
Disaster

It can be
Ignored
But it will not
Be silenced

Truth and love
Are its
Weapons
And armament

It laughs
At us
As we struggle
To outsmart it

And comforts
Us when
We come
To its terms

It asks only
That
We
Listen

So that
It
May lead
The way

GRACE

Frustratingly
Random
In times
Of necessity

As much
Absent
As it is
Observed or acted upon

Consistency
A
Constant
Challenge

The act
Of loving kindness
Brings
Awareness

Not
A pat
On
The back

Triggered
By a sense
Of
Injustice

Or by
A calling
To
Servanthood

Listening
To the softening
Of
Your heart

In the
Midst
Of a
Justifiable response

Small acts
That
Change
The world

AWARENESS

The speed
With which
Life
Passes

Forces us
To choose
Our words
Wisely

Forces us
To be aware
Of each numbered
Heartbeat

Creates sadness
With the realization
That there is always
Too much to do

Makes more poignant
The value
Of
Love

Urgently
Calls us
To
Forgive

Routinely
Makes fools
As we take
It for granted

Causes us to
Pause
In quiet
Contemplation

Makes
More precious
Sacred acts
Of grace

WALKING GENTLY

Full awareness
Causes us
To rethink our partnership
In this world

A stranger
Is
No longer
Unknown

He becomes
Unimaginable potential
Forever Linked
To Our destiny

Memories
Are
Not just
Things of the past

As much as they are
Actions
Of
The present

A
Destination
No longer
Guides us

As does
The Journey
Which begs
Our participation

Fall, spring
Or a dog
Or a cat
Or a partner

Become
Spirits
Walking gently upon the earth
Aware

Allowing the spider
To cross
In front of us
Unharmed

MY DO NOT KNOWS

I do not
Know
What I have
To offer

But
I
Will
Give

I do not know
What
To
Say

But
My
Heart
Speaks

I do not know
If I have
Comfort
To give

But
My hand

Reaches
Out

The
Laughter
Surprises
Me

The
Heartbreak
Does
Not

I go
Because
I am
Called

I do
Because
I
Am needed

I
Have
Cast
Away

My
Do
Not
Knows

DANCE PARTNERS

Their steps don't match
The music
The sway they offer
Is their own

The love and adoration
For one another
Is felt by others
As they witness

They are in their
Own world
Dancing to music
Sixty-five years old

The first dance
Was shared
The night before
Distant shores called him away

But four minutes
Was sustenance enough
For three years
Of separation

A love – now decades old
Continually
Renewing
With every step

The music is no longer
Necessary
The dance floor
Is wherever they are

We can each feel love
But this
Is what
It looks like

Teach
Me
To
Dance

MY EYES SPEAK

My voice
Is different
Than
Yours

Words
Spoken
Are
Long gone

But silence
Has
No
Hold

Look
At
My
Eyes

If you
Look away
You will
Not hear

You have
My
Permission
To stare

I
Need
To
Talk

I
Need
To be
Heard

I
Need
You to
Listen

MEMORIAL DAY

It is indeed right
To dedicate
A day
To those who have
Left their shells behind

I am humbled
As I stand
And am applauded
For the service I have performed
For my country

In church
At band stands
In prayer meetings
At banquets
At concerts

My humility is born
From the service and sacrifice
Of those who
Have served and have given
The Last Full Measure

And I am often
•Taken to my knees by the tears
In an old man's blue eyes

As he recounts the horror
Of serving in action

The tears magnify the burden on his soul
The images
Remain
Unblemished
By time

A young man hell-bent on
Glory
Became an old man
With the first pull
Of the trigger

We continually re-create
Ninety-year-old twenty-somethings
Because we don't listen
To the old man
Whose tears tell a story

We remember those
Who have left their
Burdens behind
And those who
Still carry them

GOD TAUGHT ME

My turn
To write
What I know
About God

An ice cold beer
After working hard all day
Outside on the berm
Satisfaction

The adoption of one son
The birth of another
Taken to my knees with emotion
Love

The death of a brother
Who two weeks prior
Was dancing the fox-trot
Suffering

New love
Food and sleep optional
Irrepressible energy
Passion

Dropping everything
To listen
To help shoulder the burden
Compassion

The comedian
A gin-like dry wit
An infectious smile
Laughter

Skinned knees
And disappointment
Lending you a hand to get back up
Encouragement

A pew
Taught
Me
Fear

God
Taught
Me
The rest

TEN SECONDS OF COURAGE

I had the words
But I
Did not
Speak

I was paralyzed
And yet
I was
Standing

What
Might have been
Was now
Gone

A Memory
Of my imagination
Known only
To me

Ten
Seconds
Of
Courage

To speak
To move
To act
To inspire

Throwing
Caution
To the
Wind

To
Defend
A
Stranger

To give
Voice
To
Your heart

SNOWFALL

I have
Never
Had
Cancer

But I watched
The snowfall
As if I
Had survived it

I hugged
My child
As if I
Had just been diagnosed

I watched
An
Entire
Sunset

I smelled a glass
Of wine
More than
I drank it

I Listened to
The words of a friend
As if they were
The last I would ever hear

I noticed
The second hand
On my clock
For the first time

Every kiss
Became one
To
Remember

The snowfall
Was
The most beautiful
I had ever seen.

FALL

Hello Friend
I've
Missed
You

Your crisp
Kiss
Of the cool
Morning air

The tilt of the earth
Finally working
In our
Favor

Please unpack
And
Stay
A while

Enjoy with me
That bottle of red
Held back
For your arrival

Sit with me
And take in
The beautiful paintings
You are about to create

Anticipate with me
The incense
Cut grass, campfires
Pumpkin spice

And the first
Firing
Of the
Furnace

Celebrate with me
Your many holidays
And the love
Of friends and family

Your glass is
Empty
Have
Another

THE CROWDED EMPTY SPACE

The table
Was oversized
For just
One person

One chair
Waiting
Sturdy, but
Alone

Six
Hours
Of
Interrogation

The eyes
Of
The
Questioners

Saw one
Man
One
Table

Standing
Unseen
At my side
Behind me

My mom
My dad
My brothers, sister
My teachers, friends

My confidantes
My mentors
My failures
My successes

Never once
Did I
Feel
Alone

In the
Crowded
Empty
Space

CLOSED

The sign
Was met
With
Disappointment

As I once again
Missed my chance
To get
What I needed

That I must
Wait again for the sign
To change
As I know it will

I chuckled as I
Pondered the idea
Of wearing
A sign

An unmistakable
Indication
For all
To see

"Open"
Or
"Closed"
It would read

"Closed" may be
Met
With
Disappointment

But just wait
For the sign
To
Change

I
Know
It
Will

HOPE

The
Source
Of
Sleepless nights

And the
Source
Of
Survival

It
Does
Spring
Eternal

But
Sometimes
I
Wish

It would
Just
Go
Away

And just let
An
Idea
Die
Or just let
A
Relationship
End

Instead
It holds
A loving
Embrace

Forever
A partner
To
Resiliency

And
A spark
To
Our dreams

Domesti-PUPS

DOMESTI-PUPS IS A 501c3 nonprofit organization based in Lincoln, Nebraska. Satellite locations for pet therapy programs are also located in Auburn and Omaha, Nebraska.

They provide therapy dogs, service dogs for persons with disabilities, and trained rescue dogs.

Their mission is to improve the quality of life for persons with special needs through the assistance of animals, and to promote awareness through education.

If you would like more information or wish to donate, please visit their website at http://www.domesti-pups.org/.

DR. STUART STOFFERAHN is a veteran, teacher, author and motivational speaker. He is also the founder of Nebraska Transition College, an organization that empowers individuals with an Autism Spectrum Disorder or other learning difference to be independent through employment and community support systems.

If you would like to learn more or donate, please visit www.nebraskatransitioncollege.org.

To reach Dr. Stofferahn or for booking information, please visit www.stuartstofferahn.com.

Made in the USA
Middletown, DE
30 August 2020